Author biography

Hello my fellow human. Its nice to see you here. I love how everything has led to this moment. You reading my first book ever. Thats exciting. Ive put a lot of time and effort to put this puppy together. I poured my heart and soul into putting as much information about being a successful onlyfans model. I've been in the industry for a little over two years and have made 250k in those years. I started it in my little apartment with my stepmom when I was a full time veterinary technician. I started being a sex worker because my vet tech job was getting me 1600 a month with 40 hour weeks. It was not cutting it. So there was some overlap for a couple months. I posted everyday and made content weekly. I did not skip a day. Soon my following and fan numbers grew then soon I realized I would make more money staying home. So I quit my job.That took about 4-5 months. Flash forward a year and a half, now I live in a conversion van full time. I converted it myself and vlogged the whole process. Go watch it on my youtube. I now travel the USA doing what I want whenever I want, within the laws of the government of course. I don't post or create content as much as I used to but, my youtube just started making revenue and I got my first sponsor yesterday. Soon I won't have to post nuddie pictures to support myself. And it only took a little over two years.

Secrets to a Successful Onlyfans

The easiest guide to becoming a solo social media influencer without the need for a business manager. I focus on revenue generated from onlyfans but hit some other points to make money.

Katie Dawson

ISBN 978-93-5667-062-4
© Katie Dawson 2022
Published in India 2022 by Pencil

Contributors:
Editor: Aaron Strack

A brand of
One Point Six Technologies Pvt. Ltd.
123, Building J2, Shram Seva Premises,
Wadala Truck Terminal, Wadala (E)
Mumbai 400037, Maharashtra, INDIA
E connect@thepencilapp.com
W www.thepencilapp.com

CONTENTS

Acknowledgements

Editor: Aaron Strack

Branding

- Creative and catchy brand name (how people will find you and remember you)
- Make sure your name has no resemblance to your legal name (privacy)
- Logo optional if it makes sense with your chosen name.
- Examples: JozyBlows, Reyesbaddie, Foxyshadows, Thatonegirl, Tattedbarbie

Social Media Setup

ONLYFANS

- Get verified as SOON as possible (24-48 hours) and fill out W-9 on the website

- Set Up Bank Info after your account has undergone the verification. It's very straightforward, just follow instructions provided by onlyfans.

Don't skip this. This is how we get paid! You can find this section in your profile settings under "Bank".

- <u>Profile picture</u>(NO NUDE) just a cute picture of you

- <u>Banner</u>(NO NUDE) ideally full body expose with something sexy/eye catching

- <u>BIO:</u>consists of disclaimer, what kind of content you are offering, age, height, something that makes you stand out (example - replying to ALL dms), personality description.

NOTE The most important thing about the bio is making it personal so your fans create an emotional attachment to you. THIS is what keeps people coming back.

- Subscriber welcome message IMPORTANT. Can

consist of menus, pictures, videos, short welcome paragraph, little stories about you, and various special promotions you are currently offering for them to enjoy.

NOTE This welcome message seems trivial but is VERY important, it's your first impression to your new audience member. So really try to drive your personality through this opening interaction. It could very well dictate how long someone stays or even how soon they decide to buy one of your additional services.

NOTE You can also use pictures and videos in your welcome message as an incentive to get people to subscribe. (example 1 free video the moment they subscribe)

- <u>Pricing</u>: Pricing is going to change as your following builds. So we are going to split pricing into 3 different categories, along with payment structures and strategies you can use at each level.

<u>*Beginner with 500 or less subscribers:</u>The best strategy in this situation is a 10$ subscription fee with 50% off their first month. The reason this strategy is so effective early on, comes from the fact the barrier to entry for them (5$) is very reasonable and cheap. This allows you to set the hook and pull them in to the 10$ a monthly resub following their first month.

Alternative strategy: If the prior pricing is rough and you feel you have slow growth, you can opt to lower your subscription fee to 5$ flat and after you gain a few more and hook them, return to the optimal strategy outlined above to reach our 500 subscriptions goal.

<u>*Intermediate/Advanced with 500-1000+ subscribers:</u>
1. We can start to introduce subscription bundles and promotions. This is advantageous to both you and your fans. Bundles allow you the freedom to offer a more expensive 1 time purchase and retainer fan, whilst also offering the fan a discount for forking over more dough upfront.
2. The second strategy we can introduce is promotions. There are a few strategies we can use to make the most of this feature, so we will outline a few of the most effective.

A. Choose the discount these new subscribers attain whilst participating in your promotion. Discounts can range from 5-80%, however we strongly suggest not going over a 50% discount. 40-50% discount on most occasions is optimal.

B. Now we have to choose how long we want our promotion running for. 1-30 days is the available range, it is recommended to either choose a large amount of days or a very small amount of days. Both have their advantages. Small promotion windows are good for rapid excitement and larger discounts. The goal here to try and create a feeding frenzy, a deal they can't pass up on, and barely give them any time to think about it, we want action not reaction. For longer promotions we recommend keeping the discount lower than that of your short flash promotions. longer promotions allow more time for your sale to reach large audiences, however is a more steady growth as opposed to explosive growth in the short term. ***NOTE* The key here is learning how to incorporate both into your yearly calendar to reap the benefits of**

both angles.

C. What to say in your promotional messages? Easy, staying consistent with our other themes mentioned above, it's all personality. describe what you are promoting, how it makes you feel, how it would make you feel if they decide to take you up on the promotion. **PERSONAL PERSONAL PERSONAL**. We want them to feel as though you are talking directly to them. use descriptive, meticulous, and sensual phrasing.

NOTE Promotions can be aimed at your onlyfans as a whole, or individualized and specific content that can be exclusively attained.
NOTE There is 1 other promotional option I haven't outlined yet, free trials. I don't recommend using these regularly or at all, unless used strategically. More detail about strategies involving free trials will be explained under the community collaboration section.

FANSLY

- Get verified as SOON as possible (24-48hrs) and fill out the W-9 form
- Everything for setting up is practically the same as onlyfans with the bio, welcome message, profile pic, bank info, and header.
- I made a fansly account only as a backup incase onlyfans goes under, but I wanted to give people a reason to subscribe to onlyfans and fansly so I made fansly a little different.
- I decided to make my fansly account real-time nudes and onlyfans pre-made nudes. Meaning anything taken for snap

premium, I post on the fansly page as well. Anything I take on my nice camera in a cute fit, I post on onlyfans.
- You can do it anyway you want. This is just an example.

- Now Fansly is little different from onlyfans. Fansly allows following and gives a lot more options for buying content such as subscription tiers. Imma give you an example:

Bronze: 1 nude a day $5/month
Silver: 1-2 nudes a day $7/month
Gold: 1-2 nudes a day with weekly free video release $10/month
Supreme Gold: 2-3 nudes a day with weekly free video and free dick rate $15/month
Following: teaser pics or videos to entice them to subscribe

You don't have to set it up like this. You don't have to have several subscription tiers or you can have more. I've looked at other girls on fansly and some just post and require a payment to view it. No subscription. Or its ONLY subscription. Look at other girls, get some ideas. Their profiles will come up as suggestions when you create your fansly account. Make it your own.
If you go with the different subscription tiers, remember to make separate welcome messages for each tier.

SNAPCHAT
****WARNING** DO NOT SYNC YOUR CONTACTS FROM YOUR PHONE, SNAPCHAT**

WILL ASK OFTEN, ALWAYS CHOOSE NO. YOU CAN CHANGE IN THE SETTINGS IF SAID YES.

- <u>New account:</u>Make a new snapchat with our newly found brand name. Try to get as close to it as possible. underscores, dots, and numbers also help.

- <u>Customize Bitmoji</u>, adding another layer of authenticity. might have to download the Bitmoji app for that. Make it your own to reflect your brand.

- <u>Snapchat settings:</u>

1. Navigate to the "who can" category and change contact me, send me notifications, and view my story to **EVERYONE.**

2. Under the same category make sure your "see my location" setting is turned to **ONLY ME.**

3. Same category again, under "see me in quick add" turn that setting **OFF.**

4. To secure your account, make a "GOOGLE VOICE" number (just download the app) for a free text and call number to use for snapchat phone verification.

5. Next we need to make a private story labeled "SNAP PREMIUM" to do this, click on your profile, under stories, click the button "new story" on the right side. Then click "New private story". Add your personal Snapchat to the newly created private story so that way we can just set it up with no customers yet.

6. Lastly, go ahead and set up "my eyes only" with a secure password for storing content.

LINKTREE

- Google "Linktree" and make an account with them, it's completely free to use. This is the platform we will be using in all of our social media bios to give everyone access to your various platforms. Make sure you are constantly updating the links as you add new ones!
- Down the road, I do recommend buying the premium linktree to make yourself appear professional.

INSTAGRAM
****WARNING** DO NOT LINK YOUR PERSONAL FACEBOOK ACCOUNT WITH INSTAGRAM.**
- Make a new instagram with your brand name. Try to get as close to it as possible. underscores, dots, and numbers also help. Make sure your account is set to PUBLIC and not private. There should be an option to make a new account that you can switch back and forth between without having to log in and out.

- Profile picture: Either use the same profile picture as your onlyfans account, or choose any other profile picture you like, same criteria as onlyfans, non nude, and cute.

- Bio:Has to be the pg-13 version of your onlyfans biography to prevent any instagram terms and conditions violations. However you can use phrases that don't directly disclose specifics and stay vague. For example "Get 3 free videos of your choice with your sub! Link below!" See as far as instagram knows, those are puppy videos. Just as stated before the rest of your bio just needs to be personable and about you, really not too different from your normal instagram bio.

- <u>Linktree:</u>Make sure your linktree is in your bio, that's how we funnel people from media platforms into your revenue generating platforms! There is a bio website input in instagram to copy and paste your linktree link into.

TWITTER
WARNING DO NOT SYNC CONTACTS

- Make a new twitter and use the same brand name we've been using in all of our other social media platforms. Like instagram, there should also be an option to make a new account that you can switch back and forth between without having to log in and out constantly.

- <u>Twitter Settings:</u>

- Under 'settings and privacy' go to 'privacy and safety' and make sure your account is not set to private (protect your tweets).
- Same category, under 'location' disable 'precise location' setting.
- Same category under 'safety', turn on 'mark media you tweet as containing material that may be sensitive'.
- Depending on your following, you can change your 'direct messages' settings, however as a newer or smaller content creator we recommend allowing anyone to message you.

- Now we need a <u>profile picture.</u>you can opt to use the same one that you've been using across other platforms, however twitter is far more lenient on risqué content, so if you would like, your profile picture can be a little more provocative, however we don't recommend full nudity, bc you gotta pay for the shit.

- <u>Twitter Header</u>: Follows the same sort of rules as the aforementioned profile picture for twitter, however you can just opt to use the same one from onlyfans. However doing something unique for your twitter header always adds another layer of spice for your brand. Twitter is a very big platform, and will generate a lot of traffic, so its best not to cut corners and make it as unique and vibrant as possible.

- <u>Twitter Bio:</u>This can be ALL out. I'm talking about a FULL BLOWN advertisement. You can say literally whatever buzz or sex related words with no problem. For example."15$ onlyfans - cum see high quality content from a high quality model with a high quality personality- 3 free videos with sub". This is a very shiny example of a bio, however you can get much nastier with no consequence. Make sure you also add your Linktree to your bio! That's how we funnel customers to revenue generating platforms!

TIKTOK

- Make a new account using your email or your phone number, it doesn't really matter. Just make sure you DON'T attach your Facebook account. Your email/phone number is not visible to anyone but yourself.

- <u>Username:</u>We will go into more depth about this in the tiktok section later, however we strongly recommend NOT using your brand/onlyfans name for your tiktok username.

- <u>Profile Picture:</u>Cute picture of you, not sexy or risqué. Maybe a selfie of you outdoors

- <u>Bio:</u>Has snapchat username, name, age, a short saying or cute quip, youtube link, and eventually after gaining some traction you will have the ability to put a link in your bio. This link will be your link tree link, however we will need to mask the link with bit.ly to prevent any tiktok violations or bans. We don't recommend linking your instagram. You can link your twitter account.

- <u>Video Profile:</u> A short little video of your face and you being cute. don't overthink it.

- <u>Tiktok Link:</u> To get your link for your link tree, click the top right 3 dots, go to 'share profile', then copy and paste the link into your link tree, easy peasy lemon squeezy.

REDDIT

- Make a new account using your brand name.

- <u>Avatar:</u>Just make and personalize your avatar for reddit in any way you like.

- <u>Reddit Bio:</u>Make it your own like twitter. Add your snapchat and anything else. You can promote your onlyfans directly on this platform.

- <u>Header:</u>Use the same header you are using for twitter, just make sure its not nude

- Add links to profile: onlyfans, twitter, tiktok, instagram, and whatever you want to add. They give you a list of options and only allow 5 links so choose wisely.

Equipment

NOTE Any equipment piece with an asterisk '*', is REQUIRED to have it from day 1.

- <u>Camera*</u>: Starting out with a good iPhone 8+ camera is a great start. Androids are not recommended at all, their snapchat picture quality is actual dog water. Once you have some capital you can invest in a better camera such as a Canon G7X Mark II. That camera balances quality and budget perfectly and will serve and suit any camera need we may have in the future. There are TONS of camera options out there, just choose one you're comfortable with!

- <u>Camera Stand/Tripod</u>:There are stands on amazon that can hold iphones (for when you're starting) AND regular digital cameras, so you won't have a need to get a new stand when you upgrade.

- <u>Ring Light</u>: I wouldn't say it's necessary to begin with, however once you upgrade to digital, it is a MUST. The ring light we recommend is around 150$, if you can afford that at the start, then by all means go ahead and snag one, if not waiting until you get your digital camera is perfectly fine.

- <u>Sex Toys*</u>: We recommend having a few toys on hand, definitely your choice, whatever feels best for you, just make sure there is some variety. Amazon has a great selection of devices I'm sure will do the job for just about anyone.

Examples: vibrator, dildo ranging from different colors and sizes, anal plugs (vibrating or not)

- <u>Lube*</u>: Self explanatory why you need this. We recommend water based lube for EVERYONE. makes cleanup a million times easier. Can find a bunch of brands that work just fine on amazon or your local convenient stores/sex stores.

- <u>Computer/Laptop</u>: Laptops are preferred considering they are very mobile, however if a laptop is unavailable a desktop computer will do just fine. (optional)

Wardrobe

- <u>Lingerie</u>: Can be any brand from wherever you want, I personally love SHEIN products, they're budget oriented and very good quality. Lingerie is a very large pool to play in, there are tons of options from Victorias Secret to Calvin Klein. Important thing is, find something you look and feel sexy and confident in. You're going to be recycling through them, and buying new periodically as you progress, people will want to see you in new outfits so just be cognoscente of that.

    - Outfit Ideas:
        - Cat related outfits (cat ears, tails etc)
        - Schoolgirl
        - Nurse
        - Maid
        - Video game or tv show cosplay
        - Bunny
        - Devil
        - Angel
        - Princess
        - Ballerina

- Try to stick to a certain anesthetic ie. cosplay, girl next door, bad bitch etc. Be creative.

- <u>Makeup</u>: Makeup is going to change person to person, you all probably know what looks best on you, however just in case you need some inspiration, i'll add a few simple looks down below as inspiration for your different looks.

- <u>Accessories</u>: Thigh high socks, head bands, heels, chokers, bondage accessories, masks, wips, jewelry, etc.

- **FEMALE ONLY:**I recommend having your nails done all the time. Consider it a business expense. If it suits your brand.

Market Research

Market research is entirely just about looking at other creators' content for ideas and inspiration. Let's go into a few ways we can accomplish this, and what to be looking out for.

- Constantly look at other creators' profiles, especially other creators who share the same look or style as you IE. If you're going for a pink barbie look, look for other creators who share the demographic.

- Specifically look for content they have posted that has done really well (lots of likes or retweets) and then simply replicate it.

- Another source of inspiration can be found straight up on google. Look up on google images "boudoir poses" or related search terms, and straight up copy those poses for your own content creation.

- TRENDS: Pay attention to pop culture on your various social media platforms, what tiktok sounds are other OF creators using, what types of video editing do they utilize, look for something that's easy to replicate, something easily relatable (something you can have fun w and show personality).

- Look into specific posts creators make that invoke conversation. Social media is all about interaction and the more interaction you have, the better engagement your posts will accrue. For example, used sparingly and lightly, politics is a great talking tool or anything that many people like to give their opinion about (more comments on your posts significantly boosts you in the algorithms)

- Make sure you familiarize yourself with the various rules on social media platforms so you don't get accidentally banned or put yourself in hot water. We will go into ban prevention in depth later in the "Ban Prevention" section.

NOTE stick to one side, and be true to your own opinion, don't contradict yourself. People will notice.

Side Hustles

Here we will discuss any/all other monetization techniques and platforms aside form onlyfans that can be used for extra income.

NOTESide hustles take time and in order to be profitable must be treated with the same consistency and quality as onlyfans.

Snap Premium

- Before we start, ensure you have created your snapchat and set up a private story, if you haven't, please refer back to the "Social Media Setup" portion of this guide.
- So what is snap premium? Snap Premium is a private story on your Snapchat that is only accessible to customers who pay for private access.
- Customers are only allowed access to the snaps based on their purchased package. Once time is up, access is revoked until another payment is made.
   - Packages: I recommend 3 packages available for purchase. A monthly subscription, yearly subscription, and a lifetime subscription.
   - Keeping track of subscriptions expirations: Go to your customers snapchat profile and edit their nickname to have their expiration date after their name. For example, if a Joe Dirt subscribes to your snap premium on 6/1/21 for

a month, change their name to 'Joe Dirt 7/1/21' so that way you know the exact date they expire, and each day run through the names on your list, and simply remove anyone who's subscription has expired. - For 'lifetime' subscribers, make sure you write lifetime after their name so you don't accidentally unadd them.

- Why Snap premium?

• Some countries don't have onlyfans available, however Snapchat is available worldwide

• Snapchat also provides more personal access to the creator, it feels more intimate and private to the customers bc they know you're taking these photos right then and there for them and it isn't pre made or old content. However you can post remade and old content, you can also pre take a bunch of photos and leave them in your 'my eyes only' section for later use.

- What are customers buying? Real time nudes, private conversation, videos, really anything you provide on onlyfans. Remember videos can't be longer than 1 minute due to snapchats own limitations.

Quick NoteGenerally I don't recommend doing customs or individual pictures for them to save or keep.

- When/How often should I post on SP? Generally I like to post 5 pictures to the private story in the morning and 5 posts in the evening. And if you have free time during the day you can also post a picture or two.

- What content am I posting? I'll break this into 3 categories, and it's always a good idea to try and use all the categories throughout the day.

1. Nudes - pretty self explanatory
2. Personality pictures - just pics of you going about your

day, brushing your teeth, eating food, random selfies, you get it.

3. Sexy or scandalous non nudes.

- Remember, try and utilize all 3 categories throughout the day for optimal results. People are here to get to know you and see you.

- Also post on your regular story for expired subs to see, no nude content, however it can be sexy to try and draw them back into the pay funnel. You can post a menu on your regular story as well so new potential customers know what you have to offer. We will go over menus further in the 'marketing' section

- Video calls: Customers will ask eventually if you offer video calls, we will in-depth on how to go about that, and various techniques on how to do it successfully on various platforms later in the "Livestreams" section coming up.

Payment

- How to get paid on snap premium? Payment can be through Cashapp, Squarepay, Venmo, Paypal, or Amazon gift cards. Make sure your payment methods don't have any personal identifying information. (Change your name to your initials or something if the payment platform is registered under your real name.) Remember you can only have 1 of these payment platforms each. We recommend choosing a username that sits somewhere in between your brand name and real name, so it is indistinguishable from either side so it still remains intact for personal use outside of your business.

Example: Katiedaisy (brandname) - KDdaisy (cashapp name)

- How do people find my snap premium? You will put your snap username in the content menu we will be creating further in this guide along with your other services that will be advertised on onlyfans and your other platforms.

NOTEOn snapchat is it ESSENTIAL you watermark all of your posts, to prevent any stealing of content. We will go into more depth on watermarking in the 'Legal and Taxes' Section. For real time nudes/photos use Snapchat to type your brand name somewhere it can't be easily edited or cropped out.

Live Streams

Here we will go over the different live stream options and video calls.

Onlyfans

- First thing to do is let your fans know of a live stream you are planning. You can do this via mass message, twitter post, reddit post, snapchat post, and fansly post.
- I recommend giving your fans at least a week ahead of time to plan for it. Remind your fans too.
- You can also ask your fans on onlyfans what the best time and day is to do a live stream so you get the most viewers. Then do your live stream based on that. Use the poll feature.

How to:

1. On onlyfans on the home page, there is a button labeled "go live," that is how you do a livestream. Make sure to allow video and audio when   you click it.
2. Make a description of what you'll be doing and what top tippers will get.

Example: Hello my babies! Today I'm feeling very frisky but I need a little help. Every $10 tipped I will take an article of clothing off. Once we both are down to our birthday suit, every $5, you can ask me to use or do something naughty for you. The top two tippers will get the full live stream in their DMs!

3. I feel like this is the best way to make money on a live stream. You can't just give away your content.

4. In the meantime while you're waiting for your fans to tip, try enticing them with music or dirty talk. Be yourself, don't get worked up. Remember they are fueling you to do dirty things for them. If nobody tips, try doing the live stream another time. Do not to take it to heart.

****DO NOT DRINK OR DO DRUGS ON LIVE. ONLYFANS WILL END IT****

Tiktok

- Once you get a certain amount of followers and views, you will be able to go live on tiktok. I think it's like 5-10k followers.
- Under the post option on the bottom middle, you can swipe over to the live stream.
- Create a brief header for the live stream ie. cooking, doing homework, etc.
- Then start the live stream. It can go on for however long you want but make sure to stay engaged with the viewers.
- It can be anything you want. I usually go on live streams

just to talk. This is a great way to find new followers and fans. Try to do this on the daily.

- It's a great tool. Use it.

BIG NO NOs:

DO NOTdrink or do any kind of drug on the livestream

DO NOTsay nigga or nigger (idk why but I got banned for this)

DO NOTshow any kind of nudity or imply it

DO NOTdrive while on live stream

DO NOTshow any kind of violence or hateful speech

Video calls

- Video calls can be done on snapchat, skype, or zoom. Make the accounts as needed that match your brand.

- Video calls can be fun and rewarding but please be careful. I recommend that the buyer hides their video from you so you don't have to see   them.

- **MAKE SURE TO GET PAYMENT BEFORE GOING ON VIDEO CALL**

- at least half, the other half can be paid while on video call or at the end.

- Do this to prevent getting screwed over by the buyer. **TRUST NO ONE. NO MATTER WHAT THEY SAY.**

- Cost of video calls can range, I recommend a flat fee then a per minute fee.

Example: $30 up front then $1 a minute

- The buyer can pay the upfront cost then pay the rest at the end of the video.

NOW PLEASE DO NOT SCREW OVER YOUR BUYER -meaning don't receive payment then block them before video calling. That's bad business and it will come around and bite you in the ass. Stay humble. If the video call goes well, the buyer will come back and pay you more. If your buyer is concerned about you screwing them over, tell them they can pay as soon as you get on the video call. **DO NOT START ANYTHING UNTIL YOU GET THAT PAYMENT.**If no payment is received, end the call IMMEDIATELY.

Fan Interaction

In this category, I am going to discuss how to handle your fans/followers on some of the platforms

Onlyfans
- Everyday, you are going to get DMs from your fans ranging from compliments to requests for content. Don't be afraid to be yourself with them. -
- They know you're a real person.

- Be honest with them if you don't offer the type of content they are asking. If you think you can do it, let them know you can try it the next time you have the time to make content. Or offer doing a custom for them if you want to do customs. You can charge for those more.
- If they are asking for sexting, let me know a time you can do it or be honest that you don't have time to do a session.
- You can have normal conversations with them here. I can't tell you how many fans I've helped get through their depression spell. Don't be afraid to be genuine.

Snapchat

- This will be your busiest platform when it comes to DMs.

- I recommend engaging with fans on here even if they aren't subscribed. I can't tell you how many times I talked to someone and then they subscribed because they liked me.
- Now some fans can come on strong like with a dick pic or provocative comment. Just tell them to join your snap premium or onlyfans if they wanna continue with those comments or you'll block them. If they get mad, well, they need to respect your business first. You're not there to make friends, you're there to run a business.
- Now that doesn't mean to be cold to all your fans. Be genuine to those who appreciate it. Block those who are rude and disrespectful.
- Give those not subscribed a few days to subscribe. If they don't, stop talking to them.
- Those who are subscribed to your snap premium, respond to all of their DMs when you can. Make it more personal with them. This will entice them to grow an emotional connection with you and will pay more.

Sugardaddies

- In this field, you will get lots of offers to be somebodies sugarbaby. I don't recommend pursuing that. It's more work on you and sometimes they are just scamming you (I've been scammed).
- If they won't leave you alone, block them.
- Most will ask for your real name. I recommend not giving it away, you don't wanna risk them exposing you. **DON'T TRUST ANYONE.**

Scams

- If someone is offering a large amount of money to you for the cost of nothing, IT'S A SCAM.
- If someone asks for you to send money first before receiving, IT'S A SCAM.
- **DO NOT TRUST ANYONE. THEY ARE JUST HORNY AND GREEDY PEOPLE.**
- If it smells fishy, it probably is.

Payments

Here we will discuss the several forms of payment

Venmo

- I recommend using this payment for snap premium subscriptions
- Change the name to initials or a singular name that doesn't give away your real name
- Add link to your linktree for subscribers to find easily
- When your fans send you money on this platform, make sure they make the description something vague like food, tickets, gas etc.
- Venmo doesn't like supporting onlyfans models. Try to take money out or send money occasionally to prevent getting banned. I got banned because I was receiving only money.
- They do offer a debit card that can be used to spend the money in your venmo account. I recommend getting that. It's super useful.
- Unfortunately after getting banned, you can't make another account due to being linked to paypal and paypal uses social security numbers. Trust me, I tried.
- If it's too much of a risk to get banned from this form of payment, don't use it. I haven't been using it for over a

year now and I'm doing just fine with cashapp.

Paypal

- Paypal is a little tricky. I used it for a little bit but then I got banned due to too many recurring payments.
- I don't recommend using this platform for snap premium payments due to getting banned so easily.

- As I grew my following list on twitter, I had a few people reach out to me wanting me to use their new sex toys and give a review. How it would work is they would have me choose which toy I wanna try, give me the link on amazon for it and order it. Once I received it, I left a review under the product and the seller would reimburse me for it through paypal. ONLY PAYPAL.

- I recommend keeping paypal up and running only for this purpose.
- Its a great way to get free sex toys. I did this once right before my paypal got banned.

Cashapp

- This will be your main form of payment for snap premium.
- Change your username and name into your initials or brand name. If you can make a vague name that represents your brand and real name at the same time.

Ex: $KDdaisy - katiedaisy - my real initials KD

- You can have your number, address, and email on there. Nobody will see it.
- Make sure to add a profile picture- non nude.
- Add your cashapp tag to your snap premium menu and linktree

SquarePay

- Linktree offers this form of payment

- Go to your linktree and choose the option to set up a squarepay.
- Go through the steps to set it up.

Amazon Gift Card

How to receive payment:

1. Tell your subscriber to make a gift card through their amazon account and email the gift card to themselves.
2. Once they receive it, have them screenshot the special code and send it to you.
3. Once you get the code, go to your amazon account page and click "redeem gift card."
4. Put the code in and make sure the correct amount is added to your account,
DO NOT SEND A THANK YOU. IT WILL REVEAL YOUR REAL NAME.
5 Then go back to snapchat and add the subscriber to your private story and add the date their subscription will end

behind their name.

Amazon Wishlist

- This a great way for your fans to buy you gifts easily without giving away your address or name

Setting up:

1. Go to your shopping lists in your amazon account. Make a new one labeled "gift list."
2. Add anything that you would like your fans to buy you (lingerie, toys, hobby materials, etc) to the list.
3. Once that is done, go in the gift list and click the top right three dots.
4. Then click "manage list."
5. Change the privacy to "shared."
6. Don't let Alexa manage the list.
7. Make sure the list is for "you."
8. Change the recipient name to your brand name *VERY IMPORTANT*
9. Change the email to an email that doesn't reveal your real name
10. Add your birthday and description. Personalize it to match your brand your representing.
11. Add a shipping address for your fans to send to (it wont show up on their end). Make sure to make the name on the shipping address NOT your real name.
12. Then click the option "don't spoil my surprises" at the bottom.

13. To share the link to your amazon wishlist, click the three dots on the top right hand corner again. Then "invite to list" then "view only" then "copy link." Put the link on your linktree.

14. To make sure nobody finds out your real name, make sure to change your public profile name on amazon to your brand name or fake name.

15. Go to your account settings.
16. Scroll down to "profile" under "personalized content" -click it
17. Click edit public profile.
18. Change your name. You do have the option to add a bio and other facts about you. You don't need to fill these out. Just make sure your name is changed. This is only the public name. Amazon is still aware of your real name.
19. Click save.

Collaborations

Twitter:

- After creating your twitter account, go ahead and search "katiedaisy03" and follow her. Then go under her following list and follow as many other OF girls as you can until twitter tells you, you can't follow anymore. In a few hours or just later in the day, I want you to follow more girls and do the same thing until you are following a good amount (300 AT LEAST)

- Go ahead and post a picture(s) everyday with a promotional or sexy caption. If you can't think of any, stalk some OF girls and copy their captions. It's as easy as that. You can do the same thing for content ideas ie. new angles, props, or toys.

****NOTE** I WOULD NOT RECOMMEND POSTING COMPLETELY NUDE CONTENT! KIND OF GIVES AWAY YOUR PRODUCT.**

(I know... a lot of other models do)

- You will probably notice some posts from girls that look like the following numbered examples. We will cover what each post comment means, as well as how to use them to your advantage.

1."Pinned for pinned / comment when done / I follow back "

- This is a promotional strategy used by sex workers to reach a larger audience. First if you haven't already, go ahead and pin your favorite picture tweet to your profile. How to pin your tweet:

1. Go to your tweet of your choice
2. On the top right, there are three dots, click it.
3. Then click "pin to your profile"
4. The tweet will then be at the top of all your tweets until you change it

- Next I want you to go interact with other OF creator pinned tweets (like and retweet), then comment "done" under the tweet, and don't forget to follow them. They should do the same for you and now their followers will see your post.

- Then I want you to tweet the same thing they did every few days. Check your notifications and for all the girls that commented under your post. Go ahead and retweet and like their pinned post and follow them back.

SUPPORT OTHER GIRLS SO THEY SUPPORT YOU. Trust me, you don't want them bad mouthing you.

2. "Sex worker thread / all inclusive / drop your links & promos / buyers pick / rt for support & exposure"

-This is also promotional strategy sex workers use to get their content to a larger audience. I recommend copying and pasting one of your promo or pinned tweets below any sex worker threads. Try not to retweet and like too many. Maybe just the small accounts that don't have that many retweets already.

How to copy and paste your tweet:

A. Go to your tweet

B. On the bottom right (not all the way to the corner) there is an upload symbol. Click it.

C. Click copy link

D. Go to the sex worker thread post

E. Click it and scroll down and paste the link into the tweet bar. Post it. Its like your responding to the sex worker but its actually a thread under the tweet.

- You can also create your very own sex worker thread tweet. Use the same format as the other girls. It makes your life a lot easier. Post one of those every few days.

- Another way of getting to a larger audience SWs use is "sex worker group chats." Girls on twitter create these group chats of several other sex workers and they all retweet and like their posts for each other. All they do is copy and paste their tweets in the group chat and the other girls will retweet and like it for them as long as they do the same. Now there are rules but lets go over how to get into one first.

1. Go ahead and send out a tweet saying "I'm looking to join a group chat. Is anyone looking for another member?" I would send that everyday until you get into like 3-5 group chats.

2. The girls should either comment under your post or just go ahead and DM you to join their group. Go ahead and follow any girl that reaches out to you. It shows kindness.

3. Talk to them kindly and ask to join their group. They should let you know of the rules. They really aren't strict in the rules cause it's hard to keep track but **DO FOLLOW ALL THE GIRLS IN THAT GROUP CHAT**. They

will find out if you don't and will NOT retweet your posts.The rules will be written out for you from the host.

4. Do retweet AND like all the posts that show up in the group chat. I would try to keep up with them twice a day at least. Sometimes it can get on top of you but that only means it's working as long as you're putting your daily post on there too. Do this for ALL of your group chats.

5. Try not to get sucked into any drama in the group chats. These girls can be really mean and will bad mouth you if it comes to that. I just wouldn't respond to anything that doesn't have anything to do with just retweeting and liking posts. Even when girls talk about an encounter with a buyer.

6. Now you can create your own sex worker group chat of you'd like. I wouldn't until you have at least 3000 followers cause nobody is going to want to join if you don't already have a larger audience. Same thing for getting in one but there's some nice girls out there.

7. FYI. These group chats are not allowed on twitter but we still do them. To prevent getting banned or suspended, always retweet AND like the posts. It's when you only retweet a post that it becomes a red flag.

8. If you do get sick of a group chat. Go ahead and leave it and find another if you'd like. If having 3-5 group chats is too much, you can always lessen the weight. Just leave the chats. Once you make a steady income, you wont need to do these group chats anymore. Its just for initial exposure.

Shoutout for Shoutout (SFS)- can be done on all platforms

This is when you tweet or post a girl to promote her and

she does the same for you. This can be done on all platforms: twitter, instagram, snapchat, and reddit.

- I've only used this feature on onlyfans and twitter but I recommend not doing it on onlyfans. I've noticed that my fans hate it when I do that because they are there to see me, not this girl I am promoting.

- You can reach out to girls on any platform and plainly ask them if they would like to do a SFS. Some will say "no" and thats okay, just don't take that to heart. Only because I've turned down a lot but that's only because I don't need them anymore.

- Now if they say yes, I want you to write a promotional paragraph or list about your brand and what you offer. Send over 2-3 photos for them to use and your link then they should post that for you. They will do the same for you to post. I recommend adding emojis and making it pretty and colorful so it catches buyers eyes.

- BOOM you did a SFS. I would even do it for smaller accounts at the beginning only because you are a smaller account. Once you climb the ladder, you can be more selective and try SFS with larger upcoming creators.

Like for Like (L4L)- Onlyfans

- So if you look at your onlyfans profile, at the top it will tell you how many likes you have. You want that number to be very large, so us sex workers found a way to do that without real buyers. (sneaky I know)

- You create free trials for other sex workers so they can go on your onlyfans and like all your posts and you can do the same for them. Easy. Most girls will give you a year free trial so that every time they post, you'll see it and like it for them, hence getting more likes.

- I recommend giving them a 6 month free trial so let me explain to you how to make these free trials.

1. Go to your onlyfans, click your profile on the bottom right then go to "Promotions."

2. In the middle of the screen, it will say "free trial links" with an arrow down. Click it.

3. Click "create new free trial link."

4. Put the offer limit at 10 subs, the offer expiration to none, and make the free trial duration to any amount of time you want (I recommend 6   months for SWs).

5. Once it is created, click the "copy trial link" button under that corresponding link then paste it in any DM you were in.

- Once the sex worker clicks it, they will have access to your page for that certain amount of time for free. They should go ahead and like a lot of your posts.

- You in turn, will do the same for them. Go ahead and like as many or all of their posts.

- You can do this as many times as you want with as many OF girls you'd like. If you follow too many and your feed starts getting clogged, you can unfollow them. Here's how:

1. Go to your onlyfans. Click your profile on the bottom right.

2. Click on your following list right below your name

3. Click under the corresponding page the "for free" button then "unsubscribe.

- At some point you won't have to use this strategy anymore due to having an already large amount of subs that already like your posts for you.

- Now there are other ways of collaborating with other creators. I know some onlyfans accounts with thousands of subscribers will charge you to promote you on their page. Or to put a free trial link on their page. I've never tried it but you can if you want. I recommend paying for a page that has a similar body type or style as you.

Instagram

- You can collaborate with other sex workers on instagram with a SFS or a L4L.

- Go ahead and DM them to ask if they said yes. Follow all the steps above.

- I do not recommend paying for a shoutout on instagram pages. The money is not worth it.

FYI.I do not market on here much due to being a very old platform but I always keep up with the account. Post daily.

Snapchat

- Same as instagram, you can collaborate with other sex workers on this platform via SFS or L4L.

- You can either find their snap and reach out to them or they reach out to you.

- I recommend only collaborating if the other SW has a decent amount of followers compared to yours.

- I would edit a photo and put a promotion on it with your snapchat link and onlyfans name for the sex worker to post on her story. She should do the same for you. Again find ideas from other girls on twitter if you can't think of a good promotional quote or picture pose.

- You can create/edit this photo with snapchat. <u>Here's how:</u>

1. Go to your camera view in snapchat.

2. Click the bottom left rectangles by the camera button. This takes you to your pictures on snap, your camera roll, and your Eyes Only.

3. Click 'camera roll' under the search bar. Choose a picture (non-nude).

4. Once the picture is blown up, click the top right corner three dots then "edit photo."

5. Now you can edit it however you want with filters, stickers, cropping, text, music, and a link. Play with it, you'll figure out where everything is.

6. After you're done. Go ahead and save it to your camera roll by clicking the save button on the bottom left corner.

7. Now go to the person you were snapping. On the right side of the text bar, click the two rectangles.

8. That will take you to your camera roll and snapchat memories. Make sure you click "camera roll" on the bottom.

9. Then find your saved pic (it may be where your pic that you edited is instead of it at the top of the page), click it, and send it to the person.

Content Creating Collaboration: This can be done for tiktok and onlyfans.

Tiktok

- Collaborating with other tiktokers is always good. You both get marketing content and it can be a lot of fun while also maybe making a new friend.

- I recommend meeting them in a safe environment first ie. anywhere that's public.

- Then from there you both can go somewhere to film cute tiktoks for both accounts or take pictures for instagram. It's really up to both of you.

- Again only collaborate with those that will be beneficial for you. Don't settle for a low quality content creator. You want those that stick out and are serious about the industry.

- You can make this a regular thing with this other creator.

FYI. You don't have to collaborate with other tiktokers. I know I never did and I still got to 200k followers so it's all up to what you're comfortable with.
FYI 2. If you get a weird vibe from the other creator at the public place, don't be afraid to come up with an excuse to leave or just be truthful. I would pretend my friend got in a car accident lmao.

Onlyfans

- No doubt, people are going to ask you for sex clips and for revenue purposes I would recommend making some.

- I recommend using tinder or any other dating site to find a sex partner of your choosing. I would be very honest with who you get in contact with.

- Don't put your intentions in your bio but keep it simple and sweet. Put your snapchat on there and they will go ahead and contact you there. Once they do, then you tell them what you want. Most guys are into it.

- Let them know you are OF worker that is looking for a casual sex partner that is comfortable being filmed. The camera will just be propped up so there is no need to worry about it. Also that their face will be blurred out and they do get a copy of the content.

- In this packet, I am providing you a contract sheet for you and your sex partner to sign to protect you and them. Go ahead and have them sign it before filming. Make sure they get a copy too.

- Now before actually filming, I **10000% RECOMMEND**meeting them in a public place first. Feel them out, go on a date, then if you like them, go from there. If you don't like them, leave or make an excuse ie. "Go to the bathroom."

- After filming, go ahead and edit the video with videoleap. It takes a while to blur his face throughout the whole video but it's possible.

- You can also add music or any special effects to it. I recommend cutting out any slow moving scenes of the film. You want to keep your audience hooked.

- Get your sex partners contacts and send them the unedited version of the video. In the contract it is stated he is not allowed to sell or distribute the content unless your face is blurred out. As well for you.

- I do recommend having a few sex partners at a time so you can keep up with the demand. I do not recommend one night stands. Keep the partners around. The content gets better and better the more you do it.

BUT MOST IMPORTANTLY: HAVE FUN WITH IT! THIS IS SEX WE ARE TALKING ABOUT ;)

Ban Prevention

In this section, we discuss different techniques to prevent being banned

- Given the nature of our profession, we have to take necessary precautions to preserve our social media accounts and followings. Be wary of the various platform rules, and try to adhere to them as close as you can.

- **Instagram:**No nude, no outwardly promoting your onlyfans, can't have onlyfans link in bio (use link tree or bit.ly), no menu posting, try to keep posts generally mild. Try to always have some sort of clothing on (you will get banned if you are nude but completely covered up), instagram is very generous with bans.

- **Twitter:**Do not overuse your photos, keep a variety with up to date photos. If not twitter may flag it as spam and ban. Nudes are acceptable however we don't recommend using nude content for free. Remember when interacting with other creators posts, retweet AND like, otherwise twitter might flag it as spam and ban you.

- **Tiktok:** Do not post nudes or anything related to nudity, don't even save it in your drafts, do not outwardly talk about onlyfans and don't use any erotic terminology in videos. try to keep provocative posts down to a minimum, we say 1 out of every 5 posts is acceptable. Don't post drugs or drug related content, you can talk about it, but don't show it. Don't have onlyfans or linktree link in your bio. Use twitter. I recommend making a backup tiktok account incase you do get banned.

- Do this by clicking your name at the top of your profile, then click "add account."
- Make the name of the account similar to your original. You can promote it too.

   - **Reddit:**Reddit itself is a hard platform to get banned from, what you need to watch out for is bans from specific sub reddits, in order to prevent this, simply read subreddit rules, which are usually provided for anyone to view. Some subreddits require verification and other proof, just make sure you pay close attention to the rules and what is required of you to join that subreddit to prevent any unwanted bans.

LLC Creation

LLC- Limited Liability Company

- You will need to renew your business YEARLY. I recommend adding a reminder on your phone.
- With this kind of business, you can write off all of your business expenses to the government. Meaning you don't have to pay taxes on the money you put back into the business.

Examples: lingerie, sex toys, equipment, internet, office space, makeup, clothes, shoes, transportation, photo shoots etc

To create a LLC,I recommend making it under your home state or country

1. Google "how to create a LLC in the state/country ______"
2. Several websites will come up, I recommend using the most official one that has something to do with your state or country.

Example: https://corporations.utah.gov/
3. Make sure its a government website
4. Look for a link that says "business start-up" or "registering a new business"

5. From there follow the steps. You will need to make an account under that government website. Use your legal name and all. This business is yours. Your fans will not know about this LLC.

6. Create a name for your LLC. It can be just initials or a simple word. I wouldn't use your brand name.

Examples: CCC, LLC | Animal, LLC | Makeup, LLC |

7. The name of your business will never change and once you get your business debit card, it will show up on that card with your real name on it too.

8. During the setup process, only list yourself as a member. You can add members down the road if needed.

9. Do not mention that you are selling sexual content.

10. Make your business address your home address.

11. Once you submit it, it will have to be approved (24-48hrs).

12. Once it's approved, you will get notified by email and the state will mail you your documents to the address you provided. **DO NOT LOSE THESE DOCUMENTS**. It has your EIN number (employee identification number) in it.

13. Next step is registering your LLC with your bank so you can have a business debit card.

14. You will need an Operation Agreement for your LLC. Make one on rocketlawyer.com. It will cost money. Print it and have a witness sign it with you (it can be anyone).

15. Call your bank and schedule an appointment with them to set up a business account. They should go through with you on the phone about what you need.

Legal and Taxes

Here we will discuss the process of doing your taxes every year.

- In this industry, the US government takes 20% but with write-offs, it can be much much less.
- I recommend finding a Tax Professional to do your taxes for you.
- You will need your 1099 form from onlyfans and/or fansly.

- Go to the bank icon and click at the top "To download 1099 form click here" (onlyfans)

- Don't forget to give your W-9 from any other job you participated in during that year.
- Let the Tax Pro know about your LLC. They should give you a form to fill out for all your write offs. With your business card, you should be able to fill it out using your bank statements of each month. You will have to categorize the charges by how the form is set-up. Get the right amount as close as you can.
- Remember to only look at the charges from that specific year.
- You may have to print the write off form. If you don't have a printer, print it at a UPS store or officemax. It's

super easy.

- Once it's all filled out, send a picture of it to your tax professional with all your tax forms.

- It will take a couple weeks for your taxes to be filed but once they are done. He or she should give you an amount you owe the government and the tax professional.

- The government taxes will be separated into federal and state taxes.

- You will pay via check through mail. Print the tax documents and mail them accordingly. You will be given a mailing address.

- You'll pay the tax professional anyway that professional would like. I recommend no more than $600.

****REMEMBER TO DO YOUR TAXES, YOU DON'T NEED THE IRS ON YOUR BUTT****

Business Manager

- If you're planning to do this for a while, I recommend a business manager. I used to have one but he was my boyfriend at the time so I don't have a manager anymore. With his expertise, the brand launched. We both made a ton of money. More than I could have ever made by myself. Now I am in search of a new one.
- I don't recommend finding a big company to run you. I would look for a partnership. Create a thorough contract then work together.
- I wouldn't give away anymore than 30% of your revenue and that's on the high end.
- Get somebody that knows how to market on all of the social media platforms and that can give you marketing strategies.

Mental Health

Hello, now that you've gone through the whole pamphlet of how to become a successful onlyfans model, I'm sure you are feeling overwhelmed. That's okay because it can be overwhelming. I can't tell you how many panic/anxiety attacks I've had since starting this business. It can be fun to be able to live each day the way I want to but it can be scary too because my salary is entirely based on if people subscribe to my account or not. There's a lot of reward in this industry but also a lot of sacrifice. All you need to remember is everything will be okay. Everything always works out and everything happens for a reason. I've gotten my tiktok account banned twice now. The first one at 200k followers and a short few months later, my other one at 56k followers. When I read that notification, I thought my world was ending because that's where most of my new subscribers came from. I thought I was going to plummet and have to go back to a day job, but I was wrong. I went a couple months without tiktok and I'm still making the same amount of revenue. I just decided to put my energy into my other social media platforms ie. reddit and clapper. The point is that everything will be okay as long as you stay focused and keep your mental health a priority.

Now let me tell you a story. From October to March, I was dating this guy that ended up helping me with my onlyfans. He was practically my manager slash content creator. We only dated for 5 months. The first few months were fun but he kind of wiggled himself into helping me and ended up taking half my profit on everything. We had a contract and everything (not notarized). I did love him and he loved me but he was constantly trying to degrade me for the business on tiktok. He wanted the business to launch and it made sense so I went along with it. Overtime, it started really bothering me and our relationship wasn't where I wanted it. It was very superficial with no passion. Due to us always working on the business and videotaping our sex, we never made time to be just boyfriend and girlfriend. I hated it. I ended up having my first real panic attack January 1, 2021. Then my second on February 1, 2021, then my third on February 27, 2021. All due to him. During those few months, I even communicated to him what was going on and we tried to fix it but it couldn't be fixed. I felt trapped. We had this business going and I felt like I couldn't break up with him. Then right before our Mexico trip, I sat him down and we agreed to break up. At that time, I was very unstable emotionally. I decided to take a break from the business until I was ready to come back. It ended up being two weeks of me just hanging out with my friends and family. I never posted anywhere on my platforms and before I disappeared, I told all my fans that I will be back when I'm ready. They all replied with reassurance that I need time for myself which felt great. During those two weeks, my revenue barely went down. I still made 15k that month. My point is it's okay to take a break from this business when it becomes too much. Take a day off every now and then. Do something fun and enjoy it to get away from all the stress. You need it to keep doing what you're doing. Your fans should understand if you're completely honest with them. Everybody has anxiety and stress problems, it only means you're human.

Also back to the ex boyfriend. Since our breakup, I've decided to not work with him anymore and he took it hard. He threatened to use the contract against me and was using my face in his profile pics for his tiktok and onlyfans account. His reason is I'm trying to screw him over but in reality, I want nothing to do with him. This is my business, not his. Even though he did help me a lot, it doesn't mean I owe him anything.

My point is try not to get your significant other mixed in with your business. Business and relation DO NOT mix. You can make content with each other but don't videotape EVERY time you have sex. You need those sensual times together to keep your relationship healthy. I recommend videotaping once a week if you do choose to go down this route and all the other times you have sex, DO NOT VIDEOTAPE.

If you are single like me, I recommend holding off on dating. It gets way too complicated when it's a new relationship and you're a onlyfans model. I don't want you to be taken for granted like I did. I met my ex when I was already an OF model and he jumped on the opportunity to help me and pried himself into my business then put me through a lot of pain. People can be narcissistic and will take whatever they can, especially if you're a onlyfans model. You're like a golden flower to them because not only are you a amatuer pornstar but you also own your own business and rely on nobody. PEOPLE WILL TRY TO TAKE ADVANTAGE OF YOU. Even your friends.

Jealousy may poison your friendships but that's okay. It just shows their true colors and your true friends will stick around and support you. I know it sucks losing friends but you need to realize, you are the prize. You need healthy, supporting figures around you. Not anchors that want to hold you down. Believe in yourself and people will want to be around you. Don't let just anyone into your life though. People can be sinister.

I do recommend getting a therapist if you don't already have one. I've had one and I'm getting a new one right now. It doesn't even have to be in person appointments. My therapist is in Utah and I'm in Houston. Just having a phone call weekly really helps with my sanity. Ask your friends and family if they have a therapist. Sometimes it's hard to find a good one that you like.

Overall, this is a tough industry to be in. You are going to be judged and ridiculed everyday. People are going to look down on you and think you're worth nothing but you need to know YOU ARE NOT. What you are doing is probably harder than any job half the people judging you are doing. It may not seem like it to them but you have nothing to prove. You are doing this business for yourself and only for yourself so you can live a happy, independent life while these other people are going to their 9-5 jobs that they hate. You have nothing to prove except to continue to keep the business growing. I wouldn't even react to any of the hateful comments. Just laugh at them and block them if you feel the need to. Losing a few viewers will not hurt. You need supportive viewers that will stick around and want to get to know you. Just keep believing in yourself! You are stronger than you think. Focus on your fans that support you mentally and financially.

Now I'm sure you're wondering about your family. Should you tell them or not.Well that's kind of up to you. My family does know what I do and they support me 100%. Their exact words were: As long as you're happy. My family is conservative so it did come to a shock when I heard those words come out of their mouth. At the beginning of my career, I hid it from them, probably for like 6 months. It was very difficult to hide it since I did live with my stepmom at the time. I ended up lying about my job and had to be careful to hide all of my equipment. Once I was making a good amount of money, my stepmom started noticing a shift in my lifestyle and I decided to tell her. Once she told me she still loved me, telling the rest of the family was pretty easy. My dad is a different story though, I think he knows what I do but refuses to talk about it. He never asks how I make my money and we never had a discussion over it.

Anyways I recommend waiting to tell your family until you are making a steady income with it. Now if you're only doing this for some extra cash on the side, don't tell your family. Only tell them if this ends up being your only way of income. When I told my family how much I make monthly, they became a lot more open with it. It's not like I'm out there on the streets or pole in front of horny men or women. I'm safely behind my camera in my room. Nobody knows my real name and with that, my family is safe from stalkers and interrogators.

I've been running this brand for 2 years now. It's had its ups and downs. Recently I just went through a large psoriasis breakout (skin rash) caused by my immune system. At first I was very conscious of the rash due to my job of having to take nudes everyday. I was honest with my fans and almost all of them didn't care. They said it's hotter that the rash isn't destroying my self confidence. So don't be afraid to be rejected. Be honest with your fans about anything that is going on with you. They want to get to know you, even the ugly parts.

Self-care Tips

Below is a list of things you can do when you feel yourself slipping into depression.

Self-Care Ideas for the Mind

1. Start a compliments file. Document the great things people say about you to read later.

2. Scratch off a lurker on your to-do list, something that's been there for ages and you'll never do.

3. Change up the way you make decisions. Decide something with your heart if you usually use your head. Or if you tend to go with your heart, decide with your head.

4. Go cloud-watching. Lie on your back, relax, and watch the sky.

5. Take another route to work. Mixing up your routine in small ways creates new neural pathways in the brain to keep it healthy.

6. Pay complete attention to something you usually do on autopilot, perhaps brushing your teeth, driving, eating, or performing your morning routine.

7. Goof around for a bit. Schedule in five minutes of play or fun (non-directed activity) several times throughout your day.

8. Create a deliberate habit, and routinize something small in your life by doing it in the same way each day-what you wear on Tuesdays, or picking up the dental floss before you brush.

9. Fix a small annoyance at home that's been nagging you-a button lost, a drawer that's stuck, a light bulb that's gone.

10. Punctuate your day with a mini-meditation with one minute of awareness of your thoughts, feelings, and sensations; one minute of focused attention on breathing; and one minute of awareness of the body as a whole.

11. Be selfish. Do one thing today just because it makes you happy.

12. Do a mini-declutter. Recycle three things from your wardrobe that you don't love or regularly wear.

13. Unplug for an hour. Switch everything to airplane mode and free yourself from the constant bings of social media and email.

14. Get out of your comfort zone, even if it's just talking to a stranger at the bus stop.

15. Edit your social media feeds, and take out any negative people. You can just "mute" them; you don't have to

delete them.

Self-Care Ideas for the Body

1. Give your body ten minutes of mindful attention. Use the body scan to check in with each part of your body.

2. Oxygenate by taking three deep breaths. Breathe into your abdomen, and let the air puff out your stomach and chest.

3. Get down and boogie. Put on your favorite upbeat record and shake your booty.

4. Stretch out the kinks. If you're at work, you can always head to the bathroom to avoid strange looks.

5. Run (or walk, depending on your current physical health) for a few minutes. Or go up and down the stairs three times.

6. Narrow your food choices. Pick two healthy breakfasts, lunches, and dinners and rotate for the week.

7. Activate your self-soothing system. Stroke your own arm, or if that feels too weird, moisturize.

8. Get to know yourself intimately. Look lovingly and without judgment at yourself naked. (Use a mirror to make sure you get to know all of you!)

9. Make one small change to your diet for the week. Drink an extra glass of water each day, or have an extra portion of veggies each meal.

10. Give your body a treat. Pick something from your wardrobe that feels great next to your skin.

11. Be still. Sit somewhere green, and be quiet for a few minutes.

12. Get fifteen minutes of sun, especially if you're in a cold climate. (Use sunscreen if appropriate.)

13. Inhale an upbeat smell. Try peppermint to suppress food cravings and boost mood and motivation.

14. Have a good laugh. Read a couple of comic strips that you enjoy, or watch a comedy movie.

15. Take a quick nap. Ten to twenty minutes can reduce your sleep debt and leave you ready for action.

Self-Care Ideas for the Soul

1. Imagine you're your best friend. If you were, what would you tell yourself right now? Look in the mirror and say it.

2. Use your commute for a "Beauty Scavenger Hunt." Find five unexpected beautiful things on your way to work.

3. Help someone. Carry a bag, open a door, or pick up an extra carton of milk for a neighbor.

4. Check in with your emotions. Sit quietly and just name without judgment what you're feeling.

5. Write out your thoughts. Go for fifteen minutes on anything bothering you. Then let it go as you burn or bin the paper.

6. Choose who you spend your time with today. Hang out with "Radiators" who emit enthusiasm and positivity, and not "Drains" whose pessimism and negativity robs energy.

7. Stroke a pet. If you don't have one, go to the park and find one. (Ask first!)

8. Get positive feedback. Ask three good friends to tell you what they love about you.

9. Make a small connection. Have a few sentences of conversation with someone in customer service such as a sales assistant or barista.

10. Splurge a little. Buy a small luxury as a way of valuing yourself.

11. Have a self-date. Spend an hour alone doing something that nourishes you (reading, your hobby, visiting a museum or gallery, etc.)

12. Exercise a signature strength. Think about what you're good at, and find an opportunity for it today.

13. Take a home spa. Have a long bath or shower, sit around in your bathrobe, and read magazines.

14. Ask for help-big or small, but reach out.

15. Plan a two-day holiday for next weekend. Turn off your phone, tell people you'll be away, and then do something new in your own town.
Hopefully that gives some ideas for better caring for you.